Marian Anderson

A Great Singer

Patricia and Fredrick McKissack

Illustrated by Ned O.

❖ *Great African Americans Series* ❖

ENSLOW PUBLISHERS, INC.

44 Fadem Road	P.O. Box 38
Box 699	Aldershot
Springfield, N.J. 07081	Hants GU12 6BP
U.S.A.	U.K.

For Mrs. Evelyn Glore-Ashford

Library of Congress Cataloging-in-Publication Data

McKissack, Pat, 1944-
    Marian Anderson : a great singer / Patricia and Fredrick McKissack.
    p. cm. — (Great African-Americans series)
    Summary: Tells the story of the African-American singer who struggled against prejudice to become one of the great opera performers of the century.
    ISBN 0-89490-303-9
    1. Anderson, Marian, 1902- —Juvenile literature. 2. Singers—United States—Biography—Juvenile literature. [1. Anderson, Marian, 1902- . 2. Singers. 3. Afro-Americans—Biography.]
I. McKissack, Fredrick. II. Title. III. Series.
ML3930. A5M4 1991
782.1'092—dc20
[B]   90-19163
                                 CIP
                             AC MN

Printed in the United States of America

10 9 8 7 6 5 4

Photo Credits: The Historical Society of Pennsylvania, p. 6; Metropolitan Opera Archives, pp. 18, 23; National Archives, p. 4; National Portrait Gallery, Smithsonian Institution, p. 20; Schomburg Center for Research in Black Culture/The New York Public Library/ Astor, Lenox and Tilden Foundations, pp. 14, 27; United Nations, p. 26.

Illustration Credits: Ned O., pp. 7, 8, 10, 11, 12, 16, 17, 22, 24, 28.

Cover Illustration: Ned O.

Contents

119833

Marian Anderson
Born: February 27, 1902, Philadelphia, Pennsylvania.

1

Sing, Marian, Sing

Marian Anderson was born on February 27, 1902. Her father worked on a coal truck in the winter and on an ice truck in the summer. Her mother cleaned houses. The Andersons went to church every Sunday.

Mr. Robinson was in charge of the children's **choir*** at Union Baptist

---

* Words in **bold type** are explained in *Words to Know* on page 30.

Church. Mr. Robinson invited Marian to join the choir. She was just six years old. And so began her love of music.

Marian grew up singing in church. She learned the old slave songs called **spirituals**. She sang alone and with others. Music filled her with happiness. Singing was almost as wonderful as going to the circus . . . almost.

Marian grew up in this house at 762 Martin Street. It is called a row house. These kinds of houses were all over Philadelphia's Southside in the early 1900s.

Marian's family was poor. When her father died they were even more poor. But Marian didn't mind working. She scrubbed her neighbor's front steps for a penny or two. She sang all the time. Her neighbors loved to hear her sing as she worked.

One day, Marian heard music coming

from a window. She peeked inside. A woman was playing a piano—right in her living room.

Marian was surprised. Weren't pianos found in churches? Yes. But, now Marian knew that people could have pianos in their homes, too. One day she wanted to have a piano in *her* house, she thought.

2

Mi-Mi-Mi-Mi-Mi-Mi-Mi

Marian and her sisters, Alyce and Ethel, played together and went to school together.

When they were in high school they began wondering what they would do when they were grown up. Would they be doctors? Lawyers? Teachers as their mother once had been?

More than anything Marian wanted to sing. But could a poor, black girl from Philadelphia sing well enough to make a living? Yes, she decided, it was possible.

Marian went to a nearby music school. Marian could hear singing.

Mi-Mi-Mi-Mi-Mi-Mi-Mi

"Why are you here? We don't teach **colored** people," a woman told Marian. "Go away!"

The words were unkind and mean. Marian felt bad—not for herself, but for

the woman. How could a person love music and be so filled with hate, she thought?

At last, Marian found someone who was willing to teach her—Mary Saunders Patterson, her first voice teacher. Marian worked hard to pay for her lessons. Soon she was singing her **scales**.

Then one day, Mrs. Patterson took

Marian to sing for Giuseppe Boghetti (ju-SEP-ee bo-GET-tee), a very well-known music teacher.

"I can't take a new **student**," Boghetti said. "But I will listen to her sing." Marian sang "Deep River" for him.

After hearing Marian sing, Boghetti smiled. He said she needed **practice**, practice, practice! Then Boghetti said he would take one more student: Marian Anderson.

Marian was always called *Miss* Anderson. She was married to Orpheus H. Fisher. They had known each other in school. Marian and her husband never had any children.

3

High and Low Times

Marian had happy times and sad times in her life. One very bad time came when she was twenty years old.

Marian studied very hard with Boghetti. She had sung at churches in Philadelphia. Her voice was strong. She was good— very good. Everybody said so. Why not sing in New York?

Boghetti said wait. "You need more practice."

But, Marian liked the idea of singing in

a big music hall—like Town Hall in New York City. That is where Marian had her first **concert**.

It was a terrible flop! Very few people came. The newspapers said, "Marian Anderson has a good voice . . . but she needs more practice."

Marian knew they were right. And Boghetti made her practice. She sang high

notes, low notes, and all the notes in between. Learning how to sing well was hard work.

Her practice soon paid off. Marian won a prize for singing. She got a chance

Miss Anderson always wanted to sing at the Metropolitan Opera. The person in charge of the "Met" was Rudolf Bing. Here he is showing Marian around the beautiful opera house.

to sing with the New York **Philharmonic Orchestra** in August 1925.

She was good—very good. It felt great! She sang the high notes, the low notes, and all the notes in between. She had never sung them better.

Miss Anderson sang in hundreds of cities all over the world. She became a star. But she never forgot to thank her family or her church for their help.

4

Brava! Brava!

Marian went to Europe in 1929. Her first European concert was in Germany in early 1930. People cheered for her. **Brava!** Brava! the crowds cheered.

Next Marian sang in Denmark, Sweden, Norway, and Russia. Her voice was better than ever. She was very well-known. But not many people in the United States had heard her sing. It was time to come home.

Marian's first concert was set for December 30, 1935 at Town Hall. On the boat trip home, Marian broke her leg. The show must go on, she told her family and friends.

Only a few people knew her leg was broken. This time Town Hall was full. Marian stood behind the piano. She wore a long, blue dress.

It was very quiet. The music began. Her

leg hurt, but Marian sang, and sang, and sang! When she finished, the great hall burst into cheers!

Marian sang all over the United States. She sang in the South, where black and white people were made to live separately.

One of the people who took care of Marian Anderson's business was Sol Hurok (left). He was called an agent. Here he is watching Miss Anderson agree to sing at the "Met."

They could not go to school together, work or play together. They could not sit together on buses or in music halls.

Whenever Marian sang before a crowd in the South, she bowed to the black people first. That was her way of showing she cared. It also showed that she was proud of her **race**. Brava! Brava! they cheered for her.

5

Oh, What a Morning!

Marian sang at the White House for **President** Franklin D. Roosevelt and First Lady Eleanor Roosevelt. Mrs. Roosevelt also invited Marian's mother to the White House.

In 1938, Howard University invited Miss Anderson to sing in Washington, D.C. at Constitution Hall. But the **Daughters of the American Revolution** (the **DAR**), who owned the hall, said no black person could sing there.

Marian was sad—not for herself, but for the DAR.

Other people were very angry about the way a great American was being treated. One was Mrs. Roosevelt. She left the DAR to let the world know she didn't like the way Miss Anderson was treated.

Eleanor Roosevelt (at left) and Marian Anderson became good friends. Some people, at that time, didn't think the president's wife should have black people come to the White House. But Mrs. Roosevelt did.

Then on Easter Sunday morning in 1939, Marian Anderson sang in Washington, D.C. Oh, what a morning!

She sang the **National Anthem** before 75,000 people of all races at the Lincoln Memorial. As always, a Marian Anderson concert ended with the spirituals she

After singing at the Lincoln Memorial Miss Anderson said this about Mrs. Roosevelt, ". . . she has done a great deal for people . . . I know what she did for me."

learned as a child. She sang "My Soul Is
Anchored in the Lord." It was very
beautiful. Some people cried.

In her long career, Miss Anderson won
many honors and made many records. She

sang for crowds all over the world. In 1955, she became the first African American to sing a leading part at the well-known Metropolitan Opera in New York. She also sang at the March on Washington in 1963 where Dr. Martin Luther King, Jr. gave his "I Have a Dream" speech. Oh, what a morning! She even got to sing at Constitution Hall.

A great conductor, Arturo Toscanini, said Marian had a voice heard once in a hundred years.

Marian Anderson **retired** on April 19, 1965 after a concert at New York's Carnegie Hall. She will be remembered as a person who brought people together through music.

Marian Anderson died on April 8, 1993.

Words to Know

brava—A cheer used at concerts to show the audience is happy with the singer or actor.

choir (KWY-er)—A musical group; a group of singers, sometimes in a church.

colored—An outdated name that was used for African Americans.

concert (KON-sert)—A musical show.

Daughters of the American Revolution (DAR)—A group of women whose ancestors fought in the Revolutionary War.

National Anthem—The song of a country. The national anthem of the United States is "The Star-Spangled Banner."

note—A musical sound; a music symbol that shows the musician what sound to make. When put together, notes make music.

philharmonic orchestra (fill-har-MON-ik OR-kuh- struh)—A large group of musicians who play concerts for audiences.

practice (PRAK-tis)—To go over and over something until it is learned well.

president (PREZ-i-dent)—The leader of a country or group.

race—A group of people who all share the same ancestors.

retired—To stop working.

scales—Musical sounds that move higher or lower note by note. Singers practice scales before singing.

spirituals—Religious songs that were first sung by African-American slaves.

student (STEW-dent)—A person who is interested in learning.

Index